Linda A. Brown

British Heritage Series

LONDON

Published in Great Britain 1985 by Crown Books.
CLB 1380
Crown Books is a registered imprint of Colour Library Books Ltd.
© 1985 Illustrations and text: Colour Library Books Ltd.,
    Guildford, Surrey, England.
Photographs of interiors of Windsor Castle: Crown copyright reserved.
Produced by AGSA, in Barcelona, Spain.
Printed and bound in Barcelona, Spain by Rieusset and Eurobinder.
ISBN 0 86283 337 X
DEP. LEGAL 14.890

British Heritage Series
LONDON

CROWN BOOKS

"When a man is tired of London, he is tired of life, for there is in London all that life can afford."

These famous words of Dr Johnson are as true today as when he uttered them 200 years ago. London can claim as much, if not more, variety of atmosphere, culture, entertainment, tradition and architecture as any city on earth.

Packed into the 610 square miles of Greater London – Europe's largest city – are a wealth of concert halls, art galleries, museums, parks and gardens, theatres, cinemas, restaurants and famous buildings which in recent years have drawn increasing numbers of tourists from Europe, the Far East and particularly the United States. More than ten million people now visit Britain each year and nearly all of them spend part of their holiday in the capital.

With its "bobbies", its red double-decker buses and its famous underground system among its most instantly identifiable features, London has an unhurried air of permanence reinforced by the durability of its great institutions such as the Tower, St Paul's, Buckingham Palace and Big Ben.

There is much more to London than visits to these famous tourist spots. The traveller who forsakes the guided tours for a day or two and wanders at will will come across some of the winding streets and narrow alleys so reminiscent of the city Dickens knew. One of the pleasures of London is that so much can be seen on foot – safely and without needing to walk more than two or three miles a day.

Starting perhaps from Piccadilly Circus – once regarded as the hub of the old British Empire – head south down Lower Regent Street into St James's which has remained largely unchanged for three centuries. Continue down Pall Mall to St James's Palace, built by Henry VIII as a royal residence, until Queen Victoria forsook it for Buckingham Palace at the start of her reign. But its links with the British Royal Family remain, albeit tenuously. When a new foreign ambassador arrives to take up residence in London he establishes his right to do so by presenting his credentials "at the Court of St James".

St James's also houses two of London's leading clubs for gentlemen – the Reform in Pall Mall where Jules Verne's Phineas Fogg set off to travel Around the World in Eighty Days, and the distinguished Athenaeum whose members include many Lords, Knights, Government minsters and leading figures of the arts, sciences and public life. Close by, in St James's Street itself, are two delightful old shops which have been catering to the needs of such club members for more than a century: Lobb, whose tailor-made shoes adorn the feet of royalty and the famous, and Lock's who have been making hats for more than two hundred years.

A ten-minute walk across St James's Park leads into Whitehall, where the solid facades of Government buildings look on to quiet quadrangles and discreet side streets. Even Downing Street, where the Prime Minister resides at Number Ten, has an air on an early Sunday morning of a respectable little residential street. Only the ever-present policeman at the door suggests something more significant.

Up Whitehall, into Trafalgar Square to feed the perpetually hungry pigeons and to admire the 200-foot-high Nelson's Column and Landseer's Lions, then up into St Martin's Lane where every other building seems to be a pub or a theatre. On both sides of this attractive street are a host of little courts and alleys, well stocked with specialist and antiquarian bookshops and antique dealers. In Goodwin's Court, off to the right, there are some delightful Georgian houses now occupied exclusively by people or companies connected with the arts – writers, publishers, film companies and so on.

Continue up St Martin's Lane, through Cambridge Circus and into Charing Cross Road, the centre of London's book trade, then turn left into the narrow streets of world-famous Soho.

Soho was developed after the Great Fire of London, but little of it now dates back more than a hundred years or so. It lies on the site of old hunting grounds. "So ho!" was the shout that used to go up when the hunter spotted a quarry.

Soho's chief appeal these days is not its reputation for naughty night clubs – most are nothing more than tawdry – but its cheerful cosmopolitan character.

Excellent continental restaurants, German and Scandinavian delicatessens, Italian bakers and French patisseries make it a delight for the gourmet.

Shaftesbury Avenue, at the southern end of Soho, leads back into Piccadilly Circus. Going west from there, along Piccadilly itself, there is much to see. Almost immediately on the left is St James's, a Wren Church with some superb wood carvings by Grinling Gibbons, whose work graces many fine old houses and stately homes in southern England. Further along is Hatchards, one of London's leading booksellers; and Fortnum and Mason, the food emporium with delicacies from all over the world, is always worth a visit, though the shopper on a limited budget should proceed with caution. Linger, too, to watch the wall clock outside Fortnum's with its beautiful little figures that make an appearance every hour and half hour with the clock's chimes.

On to the other – the north – side of Piccadilly and look for Albany standing back in its own quiet little courtyard away from the hustle and bustle of Piccadilly. It is a distinguished old house built at the end of the eighteenth century and now divided into exclusive apartments. One recent distinguished resident was Edward Heath, the former Prime Minister.

Further along is Burlington House, where the Royal Academy of Art stages major exhibitions, and Burlington Arcade, reputed to be the world's longest and oldest (opened in 1819) covered walk, lined by the most attractive little shops selling jewellery, militaria, perfume and examples of British craftsmanship such as woven tartan.

Down past Green Park tube station and Green Park itself laps up to the railings of Piccadilly on the South side. Here, on Sunday mornings amateur painters, from the talented to the merely enthusiastic, hang their latest masterpieces available for sale for as little as £5.

Before reaching Hyde Park Corner at the end of Piccadilly, dive down the narrow White Horse Street to the right and wander round a genuine London village – Shepherd Market – with its own distinct character formed by pavement cafés, several excellent restaurants, two or three extremely sociable pubs and some quaint little shops where personal service is the criterion of the proprietor.

Shepherd Market lies at the south end of Mayfair. Several elegant streets lead north into Grosvenor Square over which the massive eagle of the impressive American Embassy keeps beady-eyed watch. Continue north into Oxford Street but delay the shopping expedition there until you have walked up towards Marble Arch, where the Arch itself is sited close to the spot where the Tyburn Gallows dispatched many a villain in days gone by. For 600 years, until 1783, Londoners gathered here to watch public executions, a favourite form of entertainment. Cross over to the corner of Hyde Park where, if it's Sunday afternoon, you'll experience one of the great free entertainments London can offer – Speaker's Corner. Here, anyone can stand on his own soapbox and speak publicly on any subject he likes. He or she will be assured of a big audience and a lot of good natured heckling. The Corner has its own "regular" speakers who are quite accomplished, and occasionally public figures will also come to speak, subject to the same heckling as any other. But they enter the spirit of the location, giving no quarter and expecting none.

Walk back along Oxford Street, allowing plenty of time to sample the wares of what is probably the city's major shopping street. Among the tried and tested attractions are general stores like Selfridges, Marks & Spencer, John Lewis, and, for music enthusiasts, the HMV record shop that caters for every music taste from classical to jazz, rock and punk. Continue along to Oxford Circus, then turn right into one of London's most classically elegant streets – Regent Street. It was originally designed by the architect John Nash to provide the Prince Regent, later George IV, with a direct route between his palace and Regent's Park, but little of the original conception remains. However, the curving sweep of the street is still impressive and some of the shops – Liberty and Dickins and Jones among them – are London's most sophisticated.

Holborn and Bloomsbury, lying about a mile to the east of Piccadilly Circus, are well worth a visit. Here the presence of business offices is more obvious than further west but this does not detract from the area. It gives W.C.1. (west central postal region) a character of its own. It contains many places of interest – the Inns of Court, the British Museum, the University of London and numerous pleasant walks through courtyards and narrow streets. The name Holborn is thought to derive from the old English word "Bourne" meaning river or stream. The original area was a low-lying tract of ground, a hole, near the old Fleet River which now runs underground north of Fleet Street. Just to the south of Holborn (the street) lies Lincoln's Inn, one of London's four Inns of Court, the others being Gray's Inn, and the Inner and Middle Temples. Here a lawyer learns his profession, usually as a member of chambers – a firm to whom he is articled or apprenticed. Law has been practised on the site of Lincoln's Inn since the thirteenth century; although nothing remains from that time, much of the existing architecture is Tudor. Like the other Inns, Lincoln's Inn has an air of unhurried calm and tranquillity about it. Benches are dotted about the little courtyards and paths for those requiring a period of quiet comtemplation. The Inner and Middle Temples, just the other side of Fleet Street, were called by Charles Lamb " the most elegant spot in the metropolis" with their beautifully kept lawns and gardens. These inns were originally owned by the crusading Knights Templar, hence the name, and there are still strong connections and traditions dating back to the time of the Crusades. Adjoining Lincoln's Inn is Lincoln's Inn Fields, a large open square, with tennis courts and expanses of grass, occupied during summer weekdays by office workers with their sandwiches, but at weekends a quiet oasis in the heart of the city.

Further down Holborn towards Holborn Circus, a turning to the left leads into Hatton Garden where diamond merchants, some in what now look like rundown premises, carry on their lucrative trade. And further along Holborn, across the viaduct that takes the road over what was the Fleet Valley, lies Old Bailey, housing the Central Criminal Courts, where many of the most famous trials in the history of British justice have taken place. Earlier on this site stood the infamous Newgate Prison where public hangings were a frequent occurrence.

Retracing the way back along Holborn and then turning north at Southampton Row, Bloomsbury lies to the left. Bloomsbury is the literary centre of London where many publishers still have their offices. Much of the architecture is Georgian and the area houses a number of attractive squares and the two major sites of the British Museum and the University of London. Literary connections and associations are visible in almost every street, with blue wall plaques indicating the reason. Disraeli lived in Bloomsbury as a young man and the so-called Bloomsbury Set, ruled by Virginia Woolf, held court there in the 1920s.

Dante Gabriel Rossetti lived in Red Lion Square and a short distance away in Doughty Street Charles Dickens kept house for three years. It is now maintained as a museum and library open to the public.

To the south of Holborn lie the Strand (meaning "beach" which once it was to the Thames) and, where the City of London begins at Temple Bar, Fleet Street, the centre of the newspaper industry. Three major London theatres line the Strand, as well as some interesting shops, but a diversion to the north leads to Covent Garden, once the site of the famous vegetable market, now transported across the river to the Nine Elms site. Still in Covent Garden is the Inigo Jones church of St Paul's, set in the centre of a square which Shaw used for the opening scene in *Pygmalion*, later staged and filmed as *My Fair Lady*. Nearby is the Royal Opera House and the Theatre Royal, Drury Lane where *My Fair Lady* opened in London. A theatre has been on this site since 1663 but the present one dates from the early 1800s.

Between the Strand and the Thames is a pub called the Gilbert and Sullivan in John Adam Street (the area was built by the Adam brothers but little remains of their designs now). The pub has charming models of the operas dotted around its walls and mementos of W.S. Gilbert and Arthur Sullivan; very appropriate, because only a few hundred yards away, next to the famous hotel of the same name, is the Savoy Theatre where many of the original Gilbert and Sullivan operettas were first performed.

Towards the end of the Strand, and just before the Central Law Courts is the Aldwych, at which theatre the Royal Shakespeare Company had its London headquarters. And just beyond there is the church of St Clement Danes, built by Wren, which has been immortalised in the famous nursery rhyme, "Oranges and Lemons, say the bells of St Clements." Dr Johnson was a regular worshipper at the church, living a five-minute walk away in Gough Square – a turning to the left off Fleet Street leads to it. His house at No. 17 remains a fine example of Queen Anne architecture. Fleet Street itself now houses only two national newspapers, The Daily Telegraph and the Daily

Express, but most of the others, as well as many provincial newspapers, have offices in the neighbourhood.

The continuation of Fleet Street, Ludgate Hill, leads up past St Paul's and into the City of London proper. The "square mile", as it is known, stretches along the north bank of the Thames from Temple Bar to the Tower of London. It is governed by the Lord Mayor and his Court of Aldermen and even the Queen, traditionally, has to seek the Mayor's permission before entering. The City has its own police force and courts of law and during the working day upwards of half a million people earn their living there in the commercial heart of the capital. But by the weekend the City is populated by just 5,000 residents. Its street names indicate the trades and markets that used to flourish there – Bread Street (where John Milton was born), Wood Street, Ironmonger Lane and Poultry.

Near Bread Street, which runs into Cheapside, is the church of St Mary-le-Bow. To have been born within the sound of its bells – Bow Bells – is necessary for anyone who calls himself a cockney. And it was these same bells that summoned Dick Whittington back to become three times Lord Mayor, according to the legend.

Among the institutions in the City are the Mansion House, (the Lord Mayor's official residence), the Bank of England, the Monument, designed by Wren to commemorate the Great Fire of London, the Royal Exchange (no longer in commercial use but once the market place for traders in agricultural produce), and the Guildhall, where the Lord Mayor and his Sheriffs are elected. The first Guildhall was built in the early fifteenth century, but much of what can be seen now dates from the seventeenth century. Look for the memorials to two great Englishmen, Lord Nelson and Sir Winston Churchill, and the statues of two great figures of legend, Gog and Magog.

Just over the river lies the South Bank, redeveloped since World War Two and providing Londoners and visitors alike with a wealth of cultural possibilities. Nestling against Waterloo Bridge is the New National Theatre and within a few hundred yards are the National Film Theatre, the Hayward Gallery, which has a deserved reputation for presenting the best of new developments in art, and the Queen Elizabeth Hall, a concert hall specialising in chamber and ensemble music. Further along is the Royal Festival Hall, built to commemorate the 1951 Festival of Britain and now probably London's leading concert hall for orchestral and ballet works. Continuing the riverside walk, one comes to St Mary's Church tucked close beside the grandeur of Lambeth Palace. Here Captain Bligh – Bligh of the Bounty – is buried.

Lambeth Palace is the official residence of the Archbishops of Canterbury. The site dates back to the thirteenth century and landmarks of English ecclesiastical history are set there: the English prayer book was composed at Lambeth by Cranmer, conflicts of Church and State have taken place there and the evolution of the English Protestant Church has been planned and supervised there for centuries. It is not open to the public, except by appointment, but it is well worth a visit to ponder such affairs from the outside.

A walk along the South Bank is a memorable experience. The skyline on the opposite bank, with such profiles as St Paul's, Big Ben and the House of Commons clearly visible, is truly impressive. A summer's evening there with London's lights beginning to flicker on is an ideal conclusion to a first visit to the city that Heinrich Heine once described as "the greatest wonder which the world can show to the astonished spirit".

For a city whose history goes back nearly 2,000 years London has a fine display of great buildings, but because of the devastation of the Great Fire and two world wars, few of them date back further than the seventeenth century. Nevertheless, they are elegant examples of the finest architecture of their period which, combined with the people and events in their history, give them great popular appeal.

St Paul's. One of the most familiar landmarks on the London skyline, Wren's cathedral is, in fact, the fifth church on the site; the first was built as long ago as the seventh century. Work started on the current version under Wren's direction in 1675 and was completed 35 years later, by which time Wren was 78. But he lived on for another 13 years, was a regular worshipper there and is now buried in the Crypt with his tomb bearing the touchingly apt inscription: "If you seek this man's monument, look around you". The tombs of Lord Nelson and the Duke of Wellington are also to be found there, as well as alcoves in memory of musicians and writers, soldiers and sailors. Another chapel is dedicated to "the American dead of the Second World War from the people of Britain" and contains a showcase in which is a handwritten volume listing the names of all those who died during the last war. The dome of St Paul's soars 220 feet and is an inspiring sight with scenes from the life of St Paul depicted on it; and on the way up children and adults alike are ever fascinated by the whispering gallery whose rounded walls will carry the quietest of conversations round from one side to the other.

Tower of London. Steeped in history, the Tower has performed many roles, among them that of fortress (under the Normans), place of execution and torture (under the Tudors), palace, miniature zoo (Henry III kept a small menagerie there, including, so the story goes, a polar bear tethered on a piece of rope long enough to allow the animal to plop into the Thames for the occasional bite of fresh fish), and museum – which is the service it performs today. The White Tower is the

oldest part, built by William I from whitish stone brought from Normandy by the Normans. Its walls, 15 feet thick in places, were meant to, and did, resist attack. It now houses the impressive national arms museum. The rest of the Tower is medieval, with Traitors Gate and the Bloody Tower the best known features. It was at the sight of the Gate 400 years ago that Good Queen Bess, Elizabeth I of England, broke down and wept as she passed through after her sister Mary had banished her to the Tower. And it was in the Bloody Tower that the two young princes, Edward V and Richard of York, were murdered in 1483. Their bodies lay hidden for nearly 200 years until a workmen's pick uncovered them and they were reburied in Westminster Abbey. Walking from the Bloody Tower to the White Tower you pass Tower Green where many executions took place, notably those of Anne Boleyn, Catherine Howard and Lady Jane Grey. The Crown Jewels are also housed in the Tower but most of them are not as old as people think. Many of the original Jewels were destroyed by Cromwell and those on view today date from the Restoration, when Charles II had the Jewels replaced. The two highlights of the collection are undoubtedly the Black Prince's Ruby, thought to have been worn by Henry V at Agincourt in 1415 and now set in the Crown of State; and the famous Koh-i-noor Diamond (the name means mountain of light) set in the crown that was made for the 1937 coronation of Queen Elizabeth, the Queen Mother.

Westminster Abbey. The Abbey, officially the Collegiate Church of St Peter, is where most British monarchs are crowned and buried. The Cathedral, more than 500 feet long, is really in three sections – Edward the Confessor's Shrine, Henry VII's Chapel and the Commoners' Abbey. The royal tombs – among them Elizabeth I, Henry V, Mary Queen of Scots, Anne, Richard II – lie behind the altars in Edward's Shrine and Henry's Chapel, and in the former, too, is the

Coronation Chair that dates back to Edward I, with the famous Stone of Scone that has been a bone of contention between the English and the more fervent Scottish nationalists for centuries, culminating in its removal from the Abbey in 1950 (no mean feat in itself because it is extremely heavy) and eventual recovery north of the border. Henry's chapel was originally to be dedicated to his father after he had been canonized, but the Pope asked too high a sum for the dedication, so Henry changed his mind and had the chapel dedicated to himself. Poets' Corner features memorials to such great names as Chaucer, Shakespeare, Tennyson, Milton and Longfellow, and by the great west door is the famous tomb of the unknown warrior, whose body was brought back from France after the First World War.

Houses of Parliament. Apart from the majestic and echoing Westminster Hall which dates back to 1097, most of what can now be seen is no older than 140 years. It was designed in the perpendicular style after the disastrous 1834 fire which gutted the Commons, by Sir Charles Barry, who was also responsible for designing Tower Bridge. The Palace of Westminster, as it is known, covers eight acres and has nearly two miles of corridors with more than 1,000 mainly small and overcrowded rooms opening off them. Even the Chamber of the Commons, where Parliament conducts its business is, to the first time visitor, surprisingly small; and when the Chamber is crowded for an important debate MPs sit literally cheek by jowl on the open benches. When Parliament is sitting the fact is confirmed by the Union Jack flying on the Victoria Tower during the day, and at night by the light in the clock tower of Big Ben. Westminster Hall contains what is thought to be the finest timbered roof in Europe – built from Sussex oak by Richard II in 1399. It has been restored in part from time to time, on each occasion with oak from the same wood, supplied by descendants of the original suppliers.

Buckingham Palace. Until 1913 the Palace ran round three sides of a courtyard, but the fourth side, the part of the building the public now sees, was added in 1913. It was originally built in 1703 for the Duke of Buckingham who later sold it to George II for the princely sum of £21,000. The public rarely sees inside either the palace or the attractive, 40-acre gardens; the only regular access is to the Queen's Gallery, where a selection of the Queen's superb art collection is displayed, or to the Royal Mews, where the Royal coaches are stored. Chief among them is the Golden State Coach used for every coronation since George IV and, as are all the coaches, lovingly maintained by the Mews staff. The carriage horses, Cleveland Bays and Windsor Greys, are also stabled in the Mews, adjoining the harness room where the eye is caught by the glittering brasswork on such exhibits as George IV's saddle and the hand-made pony harnesses that generations of royal children have used.

The one characteristic of London that never fails to draw compliments from visitors is the extent of parkland in the centre of the city. In fact, there are more than 1200 acres of green spaces, trees, spring bulbs, and lakes within central London where it is possible to feel genuinely in the country. The noise of traffic is reduced to nothing more than a distant murmur and competes only with the buzz of summer insects to keep the visitor awake in his deckchair. In the warmer months office workers take their lunchtime sandwiches into the parks and, in the general English pursuit of the elusive sun, take any opportunity to improve their suntans. But they stay on the fringes; in the depths of Hyde Park or particularly Regents Park it is possible to find tranquil isolation with only the finches, blackbirds and squirrels for company.

Pitt the Elder, the English statesman, described the

city's parks as "the lungs of London"; the air certainly seems to smell fresher there.

The Central London parks – St James's, Green, Hyde and Kensington Gardens – provide a marvellous opportunity for a 3-mile country walk in the heart of the city. Starting from the Admiralty Arch side of St James's Park, cross in front of Buckingham Palace into Green Park; then head towards Hyde Park Corner and into Hyde Park, walking the length of it before entering Kensington Gardens. It is a delightful walk in which you need only encounter road traffic twice.

St James's Park is in fact the oldest of the Royal Parks. It was largely bog and marsh until Henry VIII had it cleared of water and stocked it with deer for hunting. More than a century later Charles II brought over to England the French landscape designer Le Notre, famous for his work at Versailles, and commissioned him to lay out a new St James's. He allowed for a lake, islands, an aviary (hence Birdcage Walk) and, on the King's instructions, a long stretch of level ground on which Charles could indulge his great passion – the French game of *paille maille*. The game has long since died out, but the name lives on alongside St James's Park, as Pall Mall. Charles also introduced various species of birds to the islands in the five-acre lake and today this area is a sanctuary, with many kinds of duck, as well as more exotic birds such as pelicans.

Green Park's 53 acres make it the smallest of the Royal Parks but with its wooded slopes it has a particular charm of its own. It once was a favourite duelling spot.

Hyde Park is perhaps the most famous of the London parks. It is a favourite place for Londoners at weekends and Bank Holidays, with the Serpentine offering swimming and boating on its tranquil but cold waters. The site was one of Henry VIII's hunting grounds and it also ran up to the infamous gallows of Tyburn (roughly where Marble Arch now stands). When Charles II came to the throne, he had the bodies of Cromwell and other Roundheads removed from their tombs in Westminster Abbey and symbolically hanged from Tyburn. A plaque records this grim event at Marble Arch.

In William III's time, Hyde Park had become notorious for footpads and felons preying on innocent passers-by. The King, who was an asthma sufferer, had moved out to the cleaner air at Kensington Palace, and decided to cut a route through Hyde Park up to the Palace, hung with lamps to keep the villains away. It became known as the *Route du Roi*, the King's way which, it is thought, is the derivation of Rotten Row where later Victorian and Edwardian gentlemen wooed their ladies on horseback.

Hyde Park, too, was a duelling site, the most famous encounter being that between Lord Mohun and the Duke of Hamilton. The Duke pierced the Lord's guard and as Mohun lay dying, the Duke bent over him to administer comfort. In his dying breath, Mohun thrust upward with his sword and both men died within minutes of each other.

These days, the Park is more peaceful; the occasional game of soccer gets a little heated, and expatriate Americans who gather on many Sunday mornings for some nostalgia with a game of baseball, are also prone to excitement.

Beyond Hyde Park going west is Kensington Gardens, where Queen Victoria was brought up as a child. In the heart of exclusive Belgravia, it has been a favourite haunt of nannies with their charges whose childhoods revolved around the famous Peter Pan statue worn smooth at the base by thousands of admiring hands; and there's the Round Pond, which attracts crowds of model boat enthusiasts.

The other major central park is Regents Park, another former Royal hunting ground that was designed by Nash for the Prince Regent and which now, with its big lake, children's pond, running tracks, sports fields and London Zoo nearby, runs Hyde Park close as a recreational centre. It also has Queen Mary's Rose Garden and the Open Air Theatre where, in good weather, fine Shakespeare productions can be enjoyed in what is almost a natural amphitheatre.

Further north are the wild, open spaces of Hampstead Heath where at holiday time funfairs abound and where, from the adjoining Spaniards Road, with its beautiful but usually crowded old Spaniard's Inn, superb views can be had as far as the Surrey and Kent Hills.

London also has its small, intimate public gardens, too numerous to list here. They can be stumbled upon most unexpectedly and are all the better for that. Usually immaculately maintained by the local authority, with manicured lawns and flower beds that seem to be a riot of colour all the year round, they also sometimes contain the ultimate compliment to their existence. On the occasional bench will be a plaque donated at the dying request of one who "spent many pleasant hours in the evening of his life" in the peace of a London garden.

London evolved as two entirely separate towns – the walled fortress founded by the Romans about AD 43 and the settlement that grew around the site of Westminster Abbey some 900 years later, the two separated by no more than a mile or two of marshy ground.

The Roman town developed after they forded the Thames between the gravel banks of what is now Ludgate Hill on the north bank and Southwark on the south, to allow their troops and transport, landing on the Kentish coast, access to their chief city, Colchester, to the north east and their further flung outposts to the north and west. Within a few years this crossing point became the hub of Roman activities in Britain, with Watling Street serving it from the south, running on north along the line of what is now the Edgware Road to St Albans and eventually to the border country, where Hadrian left his famous mark on the landscape, and other roads leading from it to feed Chichester, Silchester, Lincoln and York.

Under the Emperor Constantius, whose wife was a Briton, London flourished and at the beginning of the 3rd century AD its citizens enjoyed a standard of living that, according to historians, was not attained again until nearly 1500 years later. But it was shortlived, as was the Roman presence in Britain, and with the legions' departure the country under the Angles, Saxons and Jutes reverted to a farming economy; London was largely abandoned.

The Norman William was good for London: he rebuilt its fortifications, added the castle (now the part of the Tower known as the White Tower), had another church built on the St Paul's site (later to be destroyed by fire) and perhaps most importantly, granted a charter to the merchants of the city which laid down a measure of independence for it that the City still enjoys today in certain respects. The merchants were not slow to exercise this independence when they met at St Paul's to appoint Prince John Regent to Richard I in place of Richard's own choice whom they disliked. But John had to pay a price: in 1192 he established the city as a municipal corporation with its own mayor, later to be dignified as the Lord Mayor – an extremely influential position. Even today it is laid down that the Lord Mayor is among the first to be officially informed of a monarch's death and is traditionally the first to be summoned to a meeting of the Privy Council that announces the monarch's successor.

Just twenty years later, the City had had enough of John and forced him to sign the Magna Carta, which said specifically of the capital: "Let the City of London have all its old liberties and its free customs, as well by land as by water."

Business continued to dominate London life and not even the Black Death, from which 50,000 died and are alleged to have been buried in the "smooth-field" (the site of Smithfield), seriously halted progress. The Guildhall was completed in 1425 and by Tudor times Smithfield and Cheapside were two of Europe's chief markets where, for instance, German clocks, French wines and Venetian glassware were sold alongside British cloth.

With the arrival of Henry VIII on the throne, Westminster's destiny was uprooted. He moved the court out of Westminster Palace in favour of the Palace of Whitehall, formerly the London residence of the Archbishops of York. And with the dissolution of the monasteries Westminster Abbey became a protestant church and St Stephen's Hall the home of the Commons.

By the time the first Elizabeth was on the throne the combined population of London and Westminster was around 300,000, living largely in cramped, dirty accommodation, made no better by sewage that constantly ran down the streets from the overflowing Fleet River. This, and the continual demolition and rebuilding of these times, led to a steady stream of removals from the City to Westminster and the land between, but it was war, the Civil War of Roundheads and Cavaliers, that finally brought the unification of London and Westminster into the largest city in Europe. Earthworks were built as defence against the Royalist troops, stretching from the Tower in the east, running parallel between the Fleet and the Thames, and around the Palace of Westminster.

Twenty years later the old London disappeared, first in the Plague, which accounted for more than 50,000 lives, then in the Great Fire of 1666 which burned for four days, demolished 13,000 dwellings and left 200,000 homeless, many of them camped in the open outside the city walls.

But it gave the city fathers an opportunity which Sir Christopher Wren grasped for the redesigning of London and, although his first imaginative plan was turned down on the grounds of cost, a new London started to emerge, part of which was St Paul's, finally completed in 1710. London now stretched into Bloomsbury, and, after King William moved the court to St James's Palace, into the area north of the Palace called Piccadilly. The Strand area between London and Westminster was elegantly developed by the Adams brothers; Soho and Regent Street were put on the map and the Fleet River was covered over and condemned to an underground existence. By the early nineteenth century the Georgian era was leaving a beauty mark on the face of London: the work of Nash adorned Regent Street and Buckingham Palace, into which Victoria moved on her accession after George III bought it from the Buckingham family.

The railway reached London in 1836 and, with its rapid development, suburbia and the commuter arrived. People were able to live outside the traditional square mile and the West End, as it came to be known, and still travel reasonably cheaply and comfortably to work.

The First World War gave London a taste of aerial warfare but it was not until 1940 that the true effects were felt, when hundreds of enemy rockets and bombers filled the London sky. In those dark years 29,000 Londoners died, 240,000 houses were destroyed and major damage was caused to such buildings as Buckingham Palace, the House of Commons and Westminster Abbey. Nearly half the city's churches were devastated. The cost of re-building was terrifying and it took London nearly twenty years to obliterate most of the scars – the bomb sites that once littered the city.

London is rich in pageantry. At almost any time of the year it can be glimpsed by the discerning visitor, while to many Londoners it has become almost an unremarkable part of daily life, be it the Changing of the Guard in the forecourt of Buckingham Palace, the cheery Beefeater in his sumptuous uniform at the Tower, the Chelsea Pensioners occasionally to be seen taking the sun along the Chelsea Embankment, or even the old brewer's dray with its top-hatted driver perched high above the magnificent horse-drawn relic of Edwardian days. All these, in their different ways, are part of London's heritage.

But to most people the city's pageantry means the beautiful set-pieces brilliantly stage-managed every year in a style internationally acknowledged to be second to none; such events as the Lord Mayor's Show, the State Opening of Parliament and Trooping the Colour.

The Lord Mayor's Show. This is held on the first Saturday after the 9th November – the day on which, each year, a new Lord Mayor is elected. A long, colourful procession of carriages and floats, at times resembling more a carnival in atmosphere, winds its way through streets lined with cheering Londoners, from the Guildhall, the City's seat of government, to the Law Courts in the Strand. It is led by the new Mayor waving to his citizens from a beautiful coach built in 1757 and drawn by six magnificent dray horses. He has an escort of pikemen resplendent in the old uniforms of the Honourable Artillery Company of Pikemen and Musketeers, thought to be the oldest regiment in the world still in existence. His coach is followed by detachments from the three armed services accompanied by military bands. Each year the procession has a theme – flowers, the river, old London and so on – which is reflected in a series of beautifully designed floats put together by City associations, companies, guilds etc. The ceremony has its origins in the agreement made seven hundred years ago with King John which guaranteed the city's independence, in return for which each year the new Mayor should travel from the City to pay his respects to the Monarch. It certainly sets London alight on what is usually a damp, drizzly November day.

State Opening of Parliament. Each new session of Parliament, since the Commons has been sitting in Westminster, has been opened by a speech from the monarch of the day outlining the government's forthcoming legislative plans. The speech itself is usually remarkable for its lack of controversy or drama (it is written for the sovereign by the government of the time). But the procession to the House of Lords (the monarch always addresses her Lords with the Commons in attendance) from Buckingham Palace more than makes up for this. The Queen makes the journey in the superb Irish State Coach and is escorted by the Household Cavalry on their magnificent steeds. The short route is lined by the Brigade of Guards and the procession is, each year, Londoners' major opportunity to salute their Queen. The Opening is also marked by a 41-gun Royal Salute fired in nearby St James's Park.

Trooping the Colour. A "colour" is the ceremonial flag of a battalion or regiment, and "trooping" means marching to music. This splendid ceremony is held on the Sovereign's official birthday, the second Saturday in June (the Queen's actual birthday being 21 April). Dressed in the uniform of colonel of the regiment, she rides side-saddle from Buckingham Palace, down the Mall, turning right into Horseguards Parade just before Admiralty Arch. There she takes the salute as the scarlet-uniformed, bear-skinned Brigade of Guards (consisting of Grenadier, Coldstream, Scots, Irish and Welsh Guards), together with massed bands, put on an impressive display of precision marching. If it is a hot day it's not unusual for one or two guardsmen in their close-fitting uniforms to pass out on the parade ground, the event traditionally recorded in the following day's newspapers. But, if it is wet, the ceremony is usually cancelled because of the damage the rain would do to the costly uniforms. Trooping the Colour is said to have evolved from the time in the British Army when, at the end of the day, no soldier could be dismissed from the parade ground until the colours of the regiment were safely lodged with the Commanding Officer. Then and only then could a weary infantryman fall out and put his feet up after a heavy day's marching.

An altogether quieter act of pageantry, but no less moving, has been enacted at the Tower of London without fail every night for the past 700 years. This is the Ceremony of the Keys, in which the Tower's Chief Warder, in scarlet coat and medieval bonnet, locks the Tower and its valuable contents for the night. Admission is free but only a few people are allowed in to watch (many guide books explain how to ensure a visit).

At ten in the evening, the Tower virtually deserted, it has a moody, almost eerie atmosphere about it. One can imagine Sir Walter Raleigh pacing his cell or Anne Boleyn walking to her execution as the Warder, flickering lantern in one hand, the keys in the other, proceeds from gate to gate, turning the locks. As he approaches the Bloody Tower, a voice rings out:
"Halt. Who comes there?"
"The keys," he replies.
"Whose keys?"
"Queen Elizabeth's keys."
And after a dramatic pause, "Pass Queen Elizabeth's keys – and all's well." "God preserve Queen Elizabeth," shouts the Chief Warder; the stirring "Last Post" is sounded by a bugler and as the final note echoes away into the night the clock strikes ten, and the Tower is once more secure.

In mid-October a new legal term begins, marked by a special service at Westminster Abbey for judges, in their ermine and scarlet, and Queen's Counsels (barristers) in silk gowns. After the service they walk in stately file to the House of Lords where they have "breakfast" (actually a lunch) with the chief Law Lord, the Lord Chancellor.

These are but a few of the pageants of London which bring to those who watch them an indelible sense of the tradition and history inherent in the city.

Previous pages: the dome of St Paul's rises above the curved facade of County Hall. The ceremonial and governmental complex of Westminster (left) includes the Victorian edifice of the Palace of Westminster and the medieval Westminster Abbey and Westminster Hall. Above: pensioners in the Royal Hospital, Chelsea. Top: the Bank of England. Overleaf: (left) the Grand Staircase of Windsor Castle (picture Crown copyright reserved) and (right) the Armourers' and Brasiers' Hall.

19

PUT ON THE WHOLE ARMOUR OF GOD

Above: Chelsea Bridge, which was built in 1934 to replace one completed in 1858. Facing page: Albert Bridge, a curious structure of 1873 which combines features of both suspension and cantilever construction. Overleaf: (left) picnicking in style at Epsom Racecourse and (right) part of Harrod's famous Food Hall.

Windsor Castle was begun by William the Conqueror soon after the Battle of Hastings to protect the route to London. Over the years it has grown in size and luxuriousness to reach its present form. Above: the South Front and (facing page) St George's Chapel. Overleaf: (left) the Queen's Drawing Room and (right) the Queen's Audience Chamber (pictures Crown copyright reserved).

Left: the sleek, modern shape of Waterloo Bridge crosses the Thames beyond the railway tracks of Hungerford Bridge of 1864 and the cast iron arches of Westminster Bridge. The latter links two of the greatest administrative buildings in the country. On the south bank stands County Hall, begun in 1909 and completed in 1963, while on the north bank stands the Palace of Westminster. Above: St James's Park bandstand. Top: a Buckingham Palace garden party. Overleaf: (left) Piccadilly Circus and (right) Oxford Street.

London is nothing if not a city of pomp and ceremony. An annual display of military pageantry is the Trooping the Colour, which takes place on the Sovereign's Birthday. Each year the colour of one of the Guards Regiments is trooped, (left) that of the Scots Guards and (far left, bottom) that of the Coldstream Guards. More splendid, but rarer, are the occasions when the affairs of the Royal Family become ceremonial events. The wedding of the Prince and Princess of Wales in 1981 brought out the guards (far left, top) and the Service Chiefs (above). Overleaf: (left) the Central Lobby of the Palace of Westminster (right).

37

Top: the lightship *Nore*, in St Katherine's Dock. Above left: a city worker makes a dash for cover as rain teems down outside the Bank underground station. Above right: the Monument, built to the design of Sir Christopher Wren in 1677. The stone pillar, the tallest in the world, commemorates the Great Fire of London of 1666 and is topped by a flaming urn which was regilded in 1954, when war-time bomb damage was also repaired. Right: the Thames, flowing between the City, on the left, and Southwark, on the right. Overleaf: (left) a 'clippie' on a London bus and (right) a view of Oxford Street on a rainy day, from the top deck of a bus.

Above: the Queen's House at Greenwich, built by Inigo Jones in the 17th century and now part of the National Maritime Museum. Facing page: the Oval Cricket Ground, home of Surrey County Cricket Club, which is leased from the Duchy of Cornwall. Overleaf: St George's Hall in Windsor Castle, which was built by Edward III and enlarged five centuries later (pictures Crown copyright reserved).

Top: Kenwood House, Hampstead, an 18th-century facade on a 17th-century brick house. In 1681 Sir Stephen Fox suggested a hospital for retired soldiers to an enthusiastic Charles II. The result, ten years later, was the Royal Hospital, Chelsea (left) designed by Sir Christopher Wren. The pensioners (above) are a familiar sight in the capital in their red summer uniforms. Overleaf: (left) the 163-foot-tall pagoda at Kew Gardens, built in 1762, and (right) the Isabella Plantation in Richmond Park.

Above: a brooding sky hangs above Nelson's Column as a blimp circles overhead. Facing page: (left) the magnificent interior of the Guildhall, twice gutted by fire; first during the Great Fire in 1666 and then during the Blitz of 1940 and (right) behind the clock face of Big Ben atop the Palace of Westminster. Overleaf: (left) the Crypt Chapel and (right) the Prince's Chamber, Palace of Westminster.

Above: (right) Gog and (left) Magog, the statues of two legendary giants in the Guildhall. Top: County Hall. Right: the financial heart of the City with the black Nat West Tower. Overleaf: the Prince and Princess of Wales return to Buckingham Palace after their wedding on July 29th, 1981.

The Norman invasion of 1066 left a lasting and impressive mark in and around London. The castle at Windsor (these pages) was begun around 1078, about the same time that the massive White Tower (overleaf, right) was built. The White Tower was raised more to subdue the Londoners than to protect the city from invasion. Norman architecture can also be seen at St Bartholomew the Great (overleaf left).

When Gundulf the Monk began work on the White Tower on the orders of William the Conqueror, he was initiating a building programme which is still not complete. Every century from the eleventh to the twentieth has added to or renovated the Tower of London (right). One of the more spectacular projects of the last century was the construction of Tower Bridge (right and above) which continued the Gothic style. Overleaf: (left) a carriage on Rotten Row, Hyde Park, and (right) the King's Troop, Royal Horse Artillery, who kept their horses and full dress uniforms after mechanisation in 1946, for ceremonial purposes.

Above: Petticoat Lane, which took its name in the 17th century from the old clothes market which existed here. In the early years of this century the street was widened and the market achieved the popularity which it retains to this day. Facing page: Paddington Station, a fine iron and glass structure of 1854, which has long served as the main rail terminus between London and the west.

Previous pages: (left) the King's Dining Room and
(right) the King's Drawing Room, Windsor Castle.
The Dining Room is one of the few State Apartments
to retain the appearance given it by Charles II
during his great rebuilding works of the 1670s.
The fine ceiling was painted by Verrio while the
elaborate wood carvings are by Grinling Gibbons.
The Drawing Room lost its original decor when
George IV undertook his massive renovations in the
years after 1824. The ceiling lost its painting to
gain elegant plasterwork and decorative panels,
while the walls are hung with silk (pictures Crown
copyright reserved). These pages: the heart of
London has always been the River Thames, which
winds slowly through the city.

ondon has long been known as a sporting venue and from its earliest ays London's citizens have found diversion in sport, but the agaries of the weather often hamper the fun; (facing page) rain stops play at Wimbledon during the famous championships. Above: better weather prevails at one of the Queen's summer garden parties, which as many as 9,000 people may attend.

Above: a pub and (top left) a yacht at Richmond. Right: Admiralty Arch. Top right: Regent's Canal. Bottom right: the Albert Memorial. Overleaf: (left) Royal Hospital, Chelsea and (right) one of the State Apartments in Windsor Castle (picture Crown copyright reserved).

Crowded into the square mile west of the Tower, some of which can be seen (left) are many of the world's most important financial institutions. The graceful steel spans of Lambeth Bridge (above) were built in 1932. Overleaf: (left) the lions at the foot of Nelson's Column in Trafalgar Square, which were created by Landseer, and (right) mist and nightfall bring a touch of mystery to Parliament Square and the Clock Tower.

The various regiments of the Guards and Household Cavalry turn out in their full dress uniforms on ceremonial occasions (these pages). Overleaf: (left) the Thames at Westminster and (right) the altar and pulpit of Wren's church, St Mary-at-Hill.

83

Above left: one of London's many 'bobbies', who take their nickname from Robert Peel, the man responsible for introducing the original police force in 1829. Above right: a Guard's band on parade. Top: the modern fountain *Girl with a dolphin* by David Wynne, and Tower Bridge, whose original, hydraulic machinery for raising the bridge was preserved in 1976 when new, electric motors were installed. Right: the Albert Bridge of 1873. Overleaf: (left) mist hangs over the river at Twickenham Bridge and (right) the sun sets over St Paul's Cathedral and the City.

89

Before its move to the Isle of Dogs, Billingsgate Market (above) had been in existence from at least 1016, though it did not become exclusively concerned with fish until some centuries later.

Smithfield (right) dates only from 1638, when the City Corporation established a cattle market on the open space formerly used for tournaments and the burning of heretics and witches.

On October 16th, 1834, the Palace of Westminster
went up in flames and Parliament lost its home.
The new building (previous pages, right) was
designed by Sir Charles Barry in late-Gothic
style, but the ornamentation was the work of the
eccentric Augustus Pugin, whose elaborate design
reached its peak in the House of Lords (previous
pages, left). From the earliest days of the city,
transport was a problem and the growing population
has only exacerbated the situation (above), but
the railways have eased the problem – (top)
Liverpool Street Station and (right) Victoria
Station – as have the buses and taxis (overleaf).

London pubs (these pages) have always been centres of life for the city and each has its own character. The magnificent Waterloo Chamber (overleaf, left) in Windsor Castle was built by George IV in memory of that victory over the French and is decorated with portraits of the monarchs and soldiers who helped to overthrow Napoleon (picture Crown copyright reserved). Overleaf right: the eastern nave and choir of Westminster Abbey, the oldest part of the building, dating from the reign of Edward III, anad the elaborate screen of 1834.

Nelson's Column (above) was built with money raised by voluntary subscription and to a design by William Railton which won a competition in 1839. The great dome of St Paul's Cathedral (top and right) was almost an afterthought, for the plans originally accepted called for a spire, but Sir Christopher Wren changed the design once building had begun. Overleaf: (left) the Thames flows through rural surroundings at Richmond and (right) the astronomical clock at Hampton Court, the Tudor palace built for Cardinal Wolsey.

CLOCK COVRT

105

Richmond Park was once used for hunting, and the deer still remain (above). Facing page: the pinnacles of Tower Bridge loom through the mist above the working tugs and barges of the Thames. Overleaf:

(left) the 18th-century cellars of Berry Brothers and Rudd, wine merchants, and (right) the beautiful interior of Wren's St Margaret Pattens, one of whose pews bears the architect's initials.

The antiquity of the city can be felt at the section of Roman Wall to survive (above). The imposing wall was constructed in the late 2nd century as barbarian raids became increasingly frequent and savage. Left: St Paul's and the city. Buckingham Palace (overleaf, left) has a relatively short history as a Royal residence, but is still the centre of national rejoicing on Royal occasions (following pages). Buckingham House was bought by George III in 1762, and rebuilding was begun by George IV, who died before completion, as did William IV, Victoria being the first monarch to live in the new palace. It originally consisted of an open courtyard with the wing facing the Mall being built in 1847 and the familiar Portland stone facing not being added until 1913.

Previous pages: (left) the King's State Bed Chamber, Windsor Castle (picture Crown copyright reserved) and (right) St Paul's Cathedral. Left: the City and Southwark, looking west. Above: St Katherine's Dock and the Tower Hotel. Top: the statue of Field Marshal Smuts in Parliament Square.

The mighty River Thames (these pages) is the reason London exists where it does. The broad river allowed Roman ships this far inland while a gravel bank made a bridge feasible; where the two met the city of Londinium was founded and this joining of two important transport systems has ensured the prosperity of the city right down to the present day.

Above: the City, with the British Telecom Tower on the horizon, from the east. Facing page: (bottom left) a street stall selling shellfish, (top left) the statue of Benjamin Disraeli in Parliament Square and (right) an illuminated fountain and the Christmas tree in Trafalgar Square. Overleaf: (left) the Church of the Holy Sepulchre without Newgate, which was rebuilt by Joshua Marshall after the Great Fire and (right) the Egyptian Hall of the 18th-century Mansion House, official home of the Lord Mayor of London.

123

Throughout the turbulent Middle Ages the strongly-defended Tower (facing page) was a principal residence of the monarch, but with more peaceful times it was abandoned in favour of more comfortable and luxurious palaces, such as Hampton Court (above) 15 miles upstream on the Thames. Overleaf: (left) snow slows traffic on a London street and (right) a typical pub scene.

ampton Court Palace (these pages) was built in two main phases. In
e 16th century the jumble of brick towers, gateways and chimneys
as built to provide a fitting residence for Cardinal Wolsey, Lord

Chancellor of England. It soon became a royal residence and after
1688 William and Mary added the fine range of buildings in the French
Renaissance style with its elegant white-stone frames and details.

131

The precision manoeuvres for which the Household Division (these pages) is famous has its roots in the battlefield drills of the 18th century, when dense masses of disciplined troops were necessary for victory. Overleaf: (left) an aerial view of the Thames above Vauxhall Bridge and (right) the Palace of Westminster.

Left: a fine aerial view showing the turreted Lambeth Palace, London home of the Archbishop of Canterbury since 1200, the pinnacled Palace of Westminster and the flat expanse of Waterloo Station. Above: Kew Gardens. Top: the gates to Queen Mary's Gardens, Regents Park. Overleaf: (left) the original Big Ben, a bell of 13 tons, which sounds the hours from the Palace of Westminster (right).

The magnificent interior appointments and decoration of the Palace of Westminster are amongst the most beautiful and elaborate Gothic creations in the country. The Royal Staircase and the Norman Porch (above left) are alive with carved and gilded stonework, the Robing Room (above right), where the Queen dons the Imperial State Crown before the State Opening of Parliament, has frescoes by W. Dyce, and

St Stephen's Hall (facing page) is adorned with statues, murals, stained glass and mosaics. Overleaf left: the interior of the Apothecaries' Hall in Blackfriars Lane, which remains much as it was when rebuilt by Thomas Locke after the Great Fire. Overleaf right: the Grand Reception Room at Windsor Castle, which was built in the style of Louis XV (picture Crown copyright reserved).

140

Below: a member of the Household Brigade stands guard at Horseguards. Right: the Royal Festival Hall, a massive post-war cultural centre where recitals, concerts, films and ballets are staged to an audiences of up to 3,111. Far right,

top: the skyline of the City, with the dome of St Paul's Cathedral and the rising column of the Nat West Tower, the tallest building in Europe, which took 9 years and £72 million to complete. Far right, bottom: the Albert Bridge. Overleaf: (left) Waterloo Bridge, the cantilevered, reinforced concrete structure which replaced the old granite bridge in 1937 amid a storm of protest, and (right) a London bus.

Above: the auction rooms of Sotheby's, a company which began life in 1744 as a bookseller but is now a fine art auctioneer. Facing page: the Royal Gallery at the Palace of Westminster (overleaf left), with its mural of Wellington meeting Blucher after the Battle of Waterloo. Overleaf right: the chamber of the House of Commons, rebuilt after it was destroyed by German bombs on 10th May, 1941.

Wren's majestic edifice of St Paul's Cathedral (these pages) is the fifth cathedral to stand on this site. The first was built in 604 by St Ethelbert, King of Kent, and was accidentally destroyed by fire, as were the third and fourth, the second cathedral having been destroyed by the Vikings in 961. The fourth cathedral, known as Old St Paul's, was begun in the reign of William Rufus and was continually added to and altered until the Great Fire of 1666 destroyed it, allowing Wren to build his greatest church.
Overleaf: (left) boating on the Serpentine, Hyde Park, and (right) the Palace of Westminster.

153

Above: the daffodils of St James's Park, through which King Charles I walked on the way to his execution in 1649, with the pillared facade of Buckingham Palace in the distance. Facing page: a military band plays in Hyde Park's bandstand. Overleaf: (left) the carved oak baldacchino of the High Altar and the glittering mosaic of Christ in Majesty to be found in St Paul's Cathedral (right).

INDEX